This is an Advanced Reader Copy (Preview Only)

Q. Why have we offered this preview copy?
A. The short answer is it is a 'Powerful Selling Tool.'
Anyone trying to share or sell something knows the power of showing a little up front—just a taste to get people interested. This book preview offers you the chance to do just that.

Previews, Excerpts, and Sneak Peeks
Publishers worldwide have found that people who download and begin reading excerpts end up purchasing the books at higher rates. It provides them with an opportunity of reaching and engaging new readers and creating valuable word of mouth.

More importantly it is an opportunity to gain your honest feedback.

Please enjoy

BIANCO

BIANCO

An Italian Australian Novel

Based on Real Life events

Gianni A V Di Camillo

Copyright 2017

The moral right of Gianni Di Camillo to be identified as the Author of the work has been asserted by them in accordance with the Copyright, Designs and Patents Act 1988. All rights reserved. No part of this book may be used or reproduced by any means, graphic, electronic, or mechanical, including photocopying, recording, taping or by any information storage retrieval system without the written permission of the publisher except in the case of brief quotations embodied in critical articles and reviews.

This novel is entirely a work of fiction. The names, characters and incidents portrayed are the work of the author's imagination. Any resemblances to actual persons, living or dead, events or localities are entirely coincidental.

ADVANCED READER COPY (PART)
First edition: © Gianni Di Camillo 2017
ISBN 978-0-9876183-0-6
   (paperback - advanced reader copy only)

BOOK FORMATING
Cover design : Pickawoowoo, Laila Savolainen
Internal design : Pickawoowoo Publishing Group
Fonts: Sabon LT Std, French Script
Printed by Lightning Source (US/ UK/ AUS/ EUR)

WEB DETAILS:
www.booklaunch.io/donatopublishing/bianco

Preface

This, for all of you who are reading it, is the culmination of a rough manuscript of an idea. Many napkins, stick-it notes and envelope backs came together to formulate what very naturally became, a story.

This novel is also fundamentally a celebration of all our differences as human beings and the undeniable commonalities that bind us all. Love in one form or another, pervades the very fabric of these pages.

The story begins, of course, at the destination of my character and personality, for which I mostly have my parents, Giovanni and Giulietta Di Camillo, to thank. Their guidance and council throughout the years from the time I was a boy has sustained until the present day. They both possess a genius and harbour modest, unique, precious talent beyond words. This and, most especially included is their beauty as incredible parents, who also worked as a seamless 'family team'. A 'dynamic duo', whose love and invaluable teaching was not in combination a harsh love nor was it soft, it was what I deem as perfect.

When my nonno (grandfather), passed away all those years and seemingly lifetimes ago, the time came when, like all of us, I was about to *have* to come to terms with something. Another dish that life was essentially forcing me to digest but I could not. That is how it was for me.

Perhaps, being away from my family in the city of London amplified it, through simple isolation from a love, support and friendship base that would initially ease the pain and eventually heal, with peace of mind. An insight as to how it must have been for my grandfathers when they arrived in a foreign land which, unlike my somewhat privileged circumstances, their challenges began with English, a language that was as alien to them as the giant and monstrous, rat like creatures they first encountered called Kangaroos.

As a reluctant acceptance set in for me of my grandfathers' passing, both recent and long past, so too did something rather magical begin to unfold. Every passing day and with increasing intensity, I began to dream and wonder. I imagined to re-create scenes about both of my grandfathers and how it must have been to actually be there as the unseen, silent moving character and observer. Though this book is only based very loosely on some facets of their lives in leaving Italy and as such evolved toward the fiction I made it to be, I feel confident that I've captured the essence of their philosophies both unique to them and common to many Italian immigrants of past generations.

Many Italians who never left Italy, have little or no idea of what past immigrants experienced. Indeed many of them feel that all immigrants were luxuriated with a dream like land of plenty, devoid of hardship. Grande rumours abounded most prolifically, of what had happened to some of their countrymen in the past while in 'America'. As such, this perception amongst most Italians in Italy of opportunistic ease abroad, coined the phrase of all immigrants as *'Americani' (Americans),* who in their minds, had almost betrayed Italy at her time of need and who lived a life of luxury and could afford anything.

Although, of course, there were opportunities which they had sought to travel to places afar, equally many Australians (including recent immigrants), have little knowledge of these hardships experienced by many arriving to her shores in the 1940's, 50's and 60's. Due in great part to the propaganda of the time, there was a great deal of unwarranted suspicion, mostly toward Italians (WWII and shortly after). The world had no internet and in Australia, credit cards and 'finance' plans (certainly by modern definitions), did not exist. You either had the funds to afford what you needed or you didn't. Communication was equally difficult and frustrating....your loved ones would either receive a telegraph or more affordably, a 6 x month turn-around of a hard copy letter, especially used by Italian immigrants until the advent of international phone calls from Australia in the 1970's.

Many people are aware of the relative hardships of all immigrants from times past though and I'm confident you'll know why this story is dedicated to the memory of my *nonni* (grandfathers) and to all the immigrants across the world who dared to travel away from their homeland for a better life venturing into the unknown and who, despite extreme adversity, transcended the odds and paved the way for me, for us, to live richer lives with greater, sweeter fruits. This select, selfless group of elite individuals, did what they had to do in the almost certain knowledge that they must sacrifice themselves in order to achieve the ultimate goals for their families. How this would manifest differed from person to person, but the result was usually the same. Extreme hardship akin to a tour of a duty but for far longer, causing extreme physical and often psychological trauma, usually resulting in early death. Some and, in even more extreme parallels, *were* soldiers and/or they experienced wars in the most horrific of circumstances. I honour all of these extraordinary individuals, with a comfort for myself and for them and their memories, that their hopes and sentiments do live within me and do enliven me.

With Graciousness,
Gianni Anthony Vincent Di Camillo.

"Science is not only compatible with spirituality; it is a profound source of spirituality. When we recognise our place in an immensity of light years and in the passage of ages, when we grasp the intricacy, beauty and subtlety of life, then that soaring feeling, that sense of elation and humility combined, is surely spiritual. So our emotions in the presence of great art or music or literature, or acts of exemplary selfless courage such as those of Mohandas Ghandi or Martin Luther King, Jr. The notion that science and spirituality are somehow mutually exclusive does a disservice to both."

Carl Sagan, The Demon-Haunted World: Science as a Candle in the Dark

"You see, we are here, as far as I can tell, to help each other; our brothers, our sisters, our friends, our enemies. That is to help each other and not hurt each other."

Stevie Ray Vaughan

"World peace can be achieved when the power of love replaces the love of power"

Sri Chinmoy
Jimi Hendrix

I

Abruzzo and Campania - Italy 1950

Aloisio rose to the occasion. He knew his family would almost certainly perish here, much less have lives worth living. So with swift accuracy, he decided what must be done.

Aloisio Luciano was a rare breed. Not unlike his warrior namesake, he stood a staunch, robust figure and his temper was as notoriously cool and immaculate as his hair, already having transformed to a glistening white at age 28. An amiable enough man, who communicated through the implicitness of his actions rather than the resolution of large diluted words, unlike many of his ill-fated *picciotto* friends. Aloisio, or *Bianco (White)* as he had become known, was as permanent a fixture of the old Italy and her ways, as surely as there were ruins that adorned Rome. Although his intelligence had regularly been underestimated, he used this generally ill assessed reputation to his advantage through creative resourcefulness. Equally well, he had come to learn that the awareness of one's limitations might even prevail over the next man who bordered on genius but knew it and flaunted it. Within Aloisio's mind, this was exposure.

As he rode through the winding roads of his home state of Abruzzo then Molise and into Campania, the singing vibration of his motorcycle's cylinders seemed to stir with his thoughts. He couldn't help but reminisce of his beloved Serafina, her warm, honey lipped kisses, her delicate olive skin, her peaceful, delicate nature and her love. He could not breathe but one breath without feeling her in his heart, his mind, the very core of his being and soul.

Now, as the warm, salty sea air darted over his bullet nosed Ducati, he realised he missed Serà greater than the sum of love he possessed for his own family members combined. Though children he had, he felt almost guilty in a sense that he loved Serà with such a comparatively consuming fervour. This would forever be a question of morality within his mind, and the only cause by which he allowed the concept of mercy or indeed leniency to prevail.

Bay of Naples

In the 1950's, the bay of Naples was a rich amalgamation of continuously brewing pasta sauce scents, beautiful young lovers, countless drying laundry garments and thieves, thousands of them. They pillaged fellow Neopolitans for anything, near new underwear and jewellery included. Many of them were gypsies or *zingheri* as they were known to Italians.

Having been alerted by a man on a motorcycle, this mixed human sea parted and re-joined behind him with the fluidity of water. Aloisio's Ducati seemed to indeed travel with serious purpose, reflecting his own hard, dedicated mood with its uncompromising bullet nosed faring and relentlessly pounding motor that resonated a deep bellow which he loved. He felt connected to his machine not for speed, but for the ineffable fabric of their likenesses that bound them together. As such and though he didn't seem the least reckless, presence of this man aroused nothing less than caution, especially in approaching a crowded Napoli. As he carefully negotiated his way toward the city limits, Aloisio began a slow descent toward the bay that harboured his ship. Though in port, she appeared to drift strangely and devoid of the usual flurry of passengers and people surrounding her, she almost seemed in slumber as if awaiting exclusively for Aloisio's arrival. Her name was the '*Achille Lauro*' and she would be the Goliath that would take him across the world to what would seem another planet. These last few miles would be the last that Aloisio would ride upon the soil of his nation. The land shaped as if a boot, protruding in defiance from the remainder of Europe, especially from its mid and toward her south, where Aloisio was born and reared and where now as an honourable man, he felt he was turning his back on her. But Italy's foundation was the *famigilia (family)*. To allow them hardship without the greatest aid that he could afford them, would be an *infamità*, a cruel travesty that Aloisio hadn't done the best he could for them. His was a story he thought that was becoming so typical of post war Italy. But the young Aloisio was not so typical a man. He had already witnessed much of the world's change that was to occur in the twentieth century. Italy for some brief moments had seemed to be recovering from the war with liberty provided by the Americans and their allies.

Then, as time wore on and the allied forces departed with their '*Big Band Boogie Woogie*' and *Lucky Strike* cigarettes, Italians began to change. The opposite end to a fascist pendulum in Italy it seemed was a society where Robin Hood style bandits were commonplace. Those of them that survived the toughest post war years, naturally gravitated towards an honest *protection* system for ordinary folk against the pillaging looters and thieves. Then the looters, thievery and violence disappeared rather suddenly. Order it seemed, had been strangely restored by an unseen hand.

The Robin Hoods, once so kind had transformed themselves and their small empires into organised crime, slowly but surely. *Now that the rats were all but small in number and the problem was almost eradicated, the cats were most certainly not about to relinquish power back to the people or government.* Theirs was an ordinary way of life now. They, like poverty, had begun to consume most of this great nation like a cancer and it made Aloisio sick to his stomach. As always, he controlled his emotions by suppression. If he didn't his mind would turn to despair. That led to greater desperation and no matter how hard you tried, desperation could lead you to do irrationally desperate things, even if it was your unfortunate self. The reservoir of where these untended emotions would gather and fester, allowing for but further changes that one might never know themselves and, in a darker place. A place to draw strength from and equally, a place of inconsistent volatility....the love of power was spawned here.

Aloisio was a positive and tenacious man though and already aware of the futility of unguided emotion. He tried to comfort himself and think of the golden ticket and where it would take him, somewhere. Somewhere he could venture, make a better life, where he could be at peace and make more than enough to feed his children. Somewhere, where there could be hope for their futures. Somewhere that would give *him* the promise of hope.

As the wheel spokes of his reliable Ducati strobed flashes of warm, Neopolitan sunshine, Aloisio was slightly fearful. Might this be the last time he would ever see his beloved Italia? To feel her soothing sun massage his mind and his back as he rode his two wheeled sportster? The sweet whining of its cylinders a tribute to the passion of Italian engineers he thought. No matter, he would find his heaven on earth and after securing his world and enough money, call his wife to join him once again with the children he had left her alone to protect, *Machado, Catarì and Ettore.*

In the years to follow, Aloisio would become so hardened by the world, that he wouldn't be able to even bring himself to vocally express love. His cold nature would become notorious. For now, his heart, his mind and his lungs burned with the memory of his beloved Serà, and memories leading to his departing of her company. For now, however and until they met again, she bestowed upon him a kiss that would last as the sustenance of his love for her. He could not but exhale one breath without feeling her within him.

As their lips parted for the last time in some years, she prayed and said, "Whenever you despair, whenever you think of me, speak these words and remember they are mine. I ask the angels of light to stand at the gateway of my soul, please protect me from all negativity, except from that which I need for my learning."

That last night with his family and the following morning for Aloisio was almost unbearable. Now, riding his machine and changing its ever demanding gears was giving him clarity, but Aloisio was experiencing a turmoil of poignant emotion and in reality he staggered within, continually replaying the events of that last day, until time in his long journey became meaningless. After Serà had spoken her delicate prayer to him, he had gazed at her and, trying not to betray his anguish, he turned with a strength he was hoping could be transferred to her. The shingle under his boots turning into a creaking of fabric, vinyl and leather as he boarded the Ducati that had seen such laughter with her and the children on it. As the motorcycle squeaked slightly from his movement, it too seemed to echo his sadness which made it all the more difficult for him. Now those memories of laughter and happier times cut through his heart and he began to feel a great lump form in his throat. He gazed at his beautiful Serà and looked up at the children in their small house. They were looking down at him. Catarì was inconsolable and in her brother's arms. That was as much as Alosio could endure. He smiled at them all, his *'famiglia'*. Turning, he looked straight ahead and repositioned himself determinedly while revving the motor to life. Aloisio gently released the clutch as his Ducati sped away in a small cloud of dust toward the future.

1921 The Island of Sant'Antioco, Sardegna, Italy

Carlo slowly removed his hands from the dirt in his farm plot, a tradition of assurance and his own superstition of acquiring a wealth as rich as the volcanic dirt deposited here since before the island's history began. Ancient *Nuraghi* towers of the same culture scattered upon his land were reminders to him of another time where this organised society moved in the singular pursuit of excellence. At times he would stop work and reflect upon a people that had left nothing in vestige of writings to tell of their struggles, their austere lives or their achievements. Whenever the wind hurled vented fury from the oceans as it so often did, there could be heard a ghostly whining from the old fortified ruins. A travesty, he thought, that a people so great in having built such places of stature and organized society since before the 'bronze age', had somehow almost been erased from existence. It was rumoured that the *Nuraghi* averaged two metres or more in height, further adding to the majesty of their mystique. Great as they were (and most especially in their time and the fact that they'd lasted a thousand years), this vanished civilisation had not insured a legacy even by virtue of record. This resonated a deep echo within Carlo, of what he would never allow for his family. He could feel that with every passing day, the inevitable decision that had afflicted him for many years must very soon be made and with conviction. With neighbouring Tunisia less than a day's boat ride away, Carlo had often wondered whether that might be the answer to his plight.

It was the end of a gruelling day in the Vineyard. This side of the Mediterranean was not only drenched in Sun and heat from May until October, but the wind wrought havoc on human skin, giving Carlo characteristically hardened features, nonetheless having transfixed an almost smile like appearance upon him as kind and warm as he really was.

The day was at an end and the only help was from himself and his wife Aurora. She was a gentle creature and Carlo had never once raised his voice at her or within her presence. Her Love for him was matched only by her enterprising attitude to transcend their meagre existence. She would rise with him and make breakfast by dawn and help him in the Vineyard until 11am, when she'd carefully unwrap a basket filled with home-made fresh bread, their own delectably sweet *pomodorini* tomatoes, chilli sausage, cheese and delicious extra virgin olive oil.

While Carlo returned to work, Aurora would set about with embroidery and sewing, making over shawls for ladies, jumpers and sweaters for men and mini tapestries woven into small furniture that could often be seen in the living rooms of Sardinians. In the late afternoon she'd use the extra grapes they'd mustered to produce delicious preserves, as well as pick fruit from their private little orchard plot. These were sold every Sunday morning at the local market.

Every night Carlo and Aurora took the time to imagine wherever they might like to be in the world, dining at the best restaurant each city and town could offer. Though the couple had next to nothing, they'd made the best of their circumstances, having saved almost enough money to re-locate to Abruzzo. The town or *città* as it was called in Italy, was *Lanciano*. Carlo's brother Nunzio had already moved there with his wife three years ago and they now had a small family.

Nunzio had asked for his brother to join him and though Abbruzzo itself was as beautiful as Sardegna though in different ways, both brothers weren't pursuing the natural Apennine allure. They were the last of their family, the Lucianos. The first time they'd heard of the town's name, they both felt it no coincidence, but fate. The brothers thought it analogous of famed Romulus as the founder of Rome and, ever present in their minds, reminded them that their namesake might have something to do with the town they'd discovered....they took this as an omen of good fortune.

Preferring to stay together anyway, the Luciano brothers had, by chance of a war time friend, come into favour for work just outside the main town in *Le Serre*. The area mostly produced Tobacco leaves (and the local population usually smoked the least good rusks).

In Sardegna, the life Aurora and Carlo had made for themselves was one of simplicity and happiness and they epitomised what many before them and since have hardly acquired, a mostly happy place in this world even in having little. Both husband and wife were as in love with each other as they'd ever been. Even their weekly market run was mostly bliss. A gentle, warm walk during which he'd joke and dance, making her laugh greatly, only amplifying her love for him. For he took the courage to be whimsical, emotional and passionate in a way that most men looked down upon but secretly wished. This she thought was an immense strength, dealt with and delivered in a form that both resonated within her and massaged her spirit even when he was afar.

One particular and sparkling Sunday in May, their landlord *Catoi Lucchesu* also walked the festive market streets of the main town. He was a morose, uncouth man. Highlighted by the dark circles under his eyes and his extremely gaunt frame and un-kept wavy grey hair, he appeared as though his skeleton had been given a token of skin and thin but adequate lips with which to speak to the living. Singular respites in his behaviour announced only at the commencement of his staring glances, presented with a palpable slime, he repelled most people almost on sight. Aurora afforded him a diplomatic smile, while her insides felt as though they'd begun to creep through her skin. Carlo sensed his wife's unease immediately, though he'd predicted her reaction. He could also see that the landlord's eyes were not focussed on the wares and produce their cart displayed.

1921 The Island of Sant'Antioco, Sardegna, Italy

"Signore Lucchesu, what brings you into town on this resplendent morning?"

The landlord reacted with a half, exasperated roll of the eyes. Seemingly irritated that one might dare interrupt his inappropriate gazing. "I will never understand the need for your lengthy words Carlo. You're a farmer, not a writer. Perhaps you should go to the local bar. I hear that the English novelist, D.H. Lawrence, has come to our corner of the world and is currently basking in sun and attention. He speaks with the pacifist Don Luigi Sturzo. That will give you time to study your vocabulary and collude with your kin. Time also for me to expand my vocabulary with your wife".

Lucchesu was almost snarling gently as he looked at the ground behind the counter toward Aurora. Carlo was now becoming uncomfortable and heated and felt himself edging rapidly. He cleared his mind as best he could and remained disciplined, reminding himself to thwart the attack and appease the aggressor. That always afforded the best results with the least expense. It was why politicians could fool their followers in every election and Carlo admired at least this, amongst the governmental *pezzenovanti (big shots)*.

"Signore Lucchesu, I will be clear. Please don't mistake my kindness as my weakness. Respect for me is as a religion and I serve my life with an ethos that encourages politeness. But my wife and I are not slaves and though we serve the public, we are not servants"

Rolling his set of exasperated eyes once more, Lucchesu picked up an apple as he lectured toward Carlo with a finger. "Just make sure your finest produce is delivered on time otherwise I'll give you a lesson you'll never forget!" For centuries Italy had used the *mezzatro* concept, the arrangement being that the landlord shared half of the produce in place of having a rent paid. This ensured that the farmer could always afford the rent and the landlord would never be denied.

Carlo noticed Lucchesu assessing Aurora up and down, as she quickly moved behind her husband and held his arm. Carlo was trying to breathe calmly as the pig bit into the apple, allowing a slow drizzle of juice to escape a corner that dribbled slightly falling onto his already stained grey suit....he was definitively disgusting.

"Signore Lucchesu, we always deliver the best of our harvest on time. It seems strange that we would suddenly be late this time, does it not?"

Lucchesu the pig looked up at Carlo disdainfully and unable to reproach, snuffed loudly as he turned to walk away, frustratingly kicking up a small cloud of dust as he went.

Carlo watched and turned his head slowly as the pig trotted away. Aurora watched her husband with admiration as his face morphed from extreme alertness and concern, to an affable warmth only love could provide. With a gentle smile he took both her hands and said, "My love, it would not serve us any favours for me to fight with the man".

Aurora with her beautiful hour glass shape, jet black hair and thick African lips frowned as she turned to Carlo with a hand on one hip. With the other, she caressed Carlo's face while a gentle smile matured across her face. "*Amore,* I know you did the best thing and I feel your protection of me is always perfect. It can be decisive and yet gentle. How you stay so cool while you manage rage is beyond me, I couldn't but that strength and courage is one of the reasons I love you so".

Pulling delicately away from his wife, Carlo began

to reassemble the area of fruit that Lucchesu had so dismissively taken from, looking casual as he did so.

Aurora moved over and brushed beside him, which never ceased to arouse the most splendid of magical butterflies within him. As he stood, she placed her arms around his neck. "I think my love that your diplomacy could have served you well as an ambassador".

"Wife I'm happy to try and reason with men, but being a *Pezzenovante* of the Government is not me, nor will it ever be. I just hope you're still happy with the farmer you fell in love with?" Carlo smiled, "Maybe it was my rugged weathered looks?" They laughed heartily together, best friends always having been an element of their union.

Returning his smile, Aurora ran her fingers through Carlo's hair and he turned to reserve her outward affection. Reaching to turn his face with a possessive humour, she kissed him on the lips and stared into his soul as she whispered, "Honesty in all forms, was another reason I married you. And a real woman's heart isn't won through money, but how happy you can make her. I am that and more."

His mouth raised an almost sardonic smile. "Honesty you say? I doubt I could fool you even if I decided upon a course of innocent and occasional lies."

"This is true Donato" And she laughed the most heavenly and infectious of laughs with after smiles to match. Aurora was exactly that, a change in the atmosphere for the better with countless beautiful hues to her personality. She on the other hand, called Carlo by his middle name Donato whenever she felt the most love for him, which was often.

They were interrupted by a deluge of continuous customers toward their bounty, during which, Aurora became afflicted with enormous waves of pain from the monthly cycle.

Before finishing for the day, Carlo insisted Aurora go home to rest and recover. He preferred the lesser of two evils of her being at possible risk walking back alone, as opposed to the definitive of remaining in agonising pain while customers pestered her with noisy queries over price. Reluctantly she left on foot. The cart would be easy for Carlo to pull back home and she felt as though her insides were about to burst. Aurora wanted to crawl into a ball and fall asleep if possible.

The Thoughts of Pigs

Catoi Lucchesu was an only child who'd benefitted from his Father's real estate savvy, a business built slowly while Sardegna grew into the 20th century. Living on the south eastern point of Italy's second largest island, the Lucchesu resided in the affluence of Villasimius, where his family wanted for nothing.

Since the only buildings to sit atop the highest hills Villasimius featured, were the church and the Lucchesu residence, town folk called the mansion *Chiesa Lucchesu (Church Lucchesu)*.

Catoi's father Ambrusu Lucchesu was a philanderer, often bringing 'traveling secretaries' home and not in the least subtle concerning these follies. While his mother on the other hand, distraught with the knowledge of these goings on even within the estate, drank herself at an exceedingly exponential capacity, ever further toward her own mortality.

In arriving home one day from high school, little did the young man know what frightful terror awaited him. As he walked nearing the crest of the rise that *Chiesa Lucchesu* occupied, screams could be heard approaching the hill, alarming the young Catoi and arresting his body to a standstill.

He lifted his head toward a dark winter's sky as if to pose a question toward the gods what the matter might be. Several staff suddenly ran madly past him, leaving Master Lucchesu aghast and with a distinctly melancholic feeling amid a sea of acrid bile he began to taste in his mouth. The house he remembered his father romancing his mother within seemed to transform instantaneously with the lack of light from above. It grew cold and foreboding. Rather than the front door being opened by the chirpy maids on return to his parents' house, the entrance had been abandoned by his witness of the mass exodus of the villa's staff. Catoi feared to enter the residence again, with an almost secure knowledge of what lay within.

The lady of the house, Valeria Lucchesu was in the only state she'd grown accustomed to surviving these days. One where everything ended with a bottle of anything that would drown the disappointment of her life. First with having had her marriage pre-ordained, to a man she knew nothing of. Then with his voracious sexual appetite demanded upon her person, which inevitably, partly through his nature and partly due to Valeria's inexperience, led toward his flirtations and adultery.

That day saw Catoi Lucchesu discover his mother, a large bloodied knife in hand, sitting and staring at his father's body strewn facedown. The same day saw Catoi having to answer questions by the *polizia* regarding what he'd witnessed and then lawyers, regarding the estate and his father's will.

As Catoi's mother was carted to a psychiatric hospital, Catoi had been obliged to settle his family's affairs. Ambrusu had seen to his son's needs, should anything ever happen to him.

Despite the vast business empire, countless properties and investments left to him by the estate, Catoi struggled to maintain his father's presence. Rather than being diplomatically charming as Ambrusu was (a man who seemed to attract good energy and electrify people), Catoi was socially inept and awkward. His presence had the opposite effect, dispersing whatever good atmosphere there already was. People mistrusted him in business dealings and it wasn't just his inexperience, it was comments, often juxtaposed and out of context. There were many times where Catoi would laugh at whatever demented version of humour he understood, while no one else even smiled. He evoked in people a sense of embarrassment for him and were it not for his family history, they would not even afford him their regular sullen glances toward the ground. Whatever favours his father had still been owed were now decidedly forgotten.

Further darkened at peoples' continuous rumours, Catoi could often hear his name whispered and aptly, his reputation had become likened to a scurrying, dirty rat.

Many women were initially attracted by the money and power, but even they couldn't endure Catoi's strange loquacious rants at the most inopportune moments, often laced with ghastly undertones.

His one saving grace was his utter bitterness toward the world. The father he'd only begun to know and understand was now gone and his guidance with it. His mother who he had thought so demure yet loving, had committed murder toward the man that held their world together, no doubt exacerbated by her incessant drinking at having to endure her husband's greatest vice.

With this vicious circle of tragedy, began Catoi's burden and paradoxically, a contorted sense of strength. His attempting to make sense of things got him no further than re-running that fateful day over and over in his mind. The more he ran these scenes, the closer he edged toward madness.

Through his ordeal in younger life, affording him psychological damage in later life, Catoi subverted the slightest female companionship and friendship. He was alone. All this fuelled his utter ruthlessness. But he was erratic, out of control and not possessing his father's patience or ambassadorial talent. Instead, he had inherited Ambrusu's flamboyance in his penchant lust for women, with a psychosis that lacked compassion, not because he didn't care, but because he no longer had any capacity for it. Catoi Lucchesu was as dangerous to himself as he was to others. Unfortunately, Aurora and Carlo Luciano were on his radar and *mezzatro* list. Now roused by Carlo's audacity, Catoi's wanton feelings toward Aurora were increasing with pressured intensity.

Having loitered at nearby stalls, he couldn't believe his luck when he saw Aurora walk away with her handbag, obviously with no intention of returning at least for a while. She didn't walk with her usual elegance. Instead she seemed distracted and stooped, almost tripping over herself. Catoi was greatly satisfied at this apparent and highly irregular vulnerability in *Signora* Luciano.

Aurora walked the first parts of the road, past the town square and away toward the ocean. Hardly having the energy to move without laying down right there, it was a battle to muster the slightest smile as she almost careened past town folk and families she knew. Even so, she had an uneasy feeling and an overwhelming sense that she was being followed, but her pain took over and she dismissed it.

Carlo, though a little worried about Aurora, was still looking forward to seeing her when he would arrive home. While on one hand they were secretly scheduled to leave for Abbruzzo in a few months, that nagging feeling, of needing a solution to their ever growing problem, had just been brought out of slumber by Catoi the landlord's recent behaviour. Aloisio detested having to stay on his guard but knew the personality of the man in question warranted at least this. Fading back from his thoughts into the present, an agitated customer in the form of an old lady had been asking him a price for a bag of peaches, which he affably answered in bargain. When Aloisio returned her change with a smile, he noticed Catoi the pig in the background, slide creepily past people with a strange walk and in the direction Aurora had taken.

A man might walk languidly without a care in the world. He also might walk with a sense of purpose. Mr. Catoi Lucchesu was traveling differently with the unmistakable sense of deliberate and imminent action. It appeared as though he was exercising stealth. A sense of adrenalin pierced Aloisio's heart like a knife. Though he knew his wife was perhaps 500 metres ahead, there was enough of a proximity between her and the pig, to incite great concern within Aloisio.

He packed his cart, though trying not to look too rushed. When he started to head in the same direction as his wife, he estimated he might be as far as 1 km behind Lucchesu. He began to move swiftly even dispensing warm hello's when needed, running as fast as his cart would allow though not so fast as to attract any real attention.

Aurora was in agony and the rocky paths along the coast that had led her home didn't make the going any easier. After a few more minutes with the sun exacerbating her feeling of extreme nausea, Aurora decided to sit down near a lone olive tree for a short rest.

She tried to calm herself in the shade and think good thoughts of Carlo and the lover within her husband, as well as the gentle and best friend all within the person she married. Aurora first met Carlo when she was 19 years old, in her home town of Santa Marina on the Aeolian island of Salina. Sicily's main most archipelago was borne from the existence of Volcanoes both active and past. Sicilians were as notoriously dangerous as they were generous, hospitable and loving. Though it was said even by main land Sicilians, that the people from these islands were originally cast by their volcanic geography in being volatile and literally explosive in emotion. If southern Italy seemed to defy Rome and the north, then these specks of land in the sea epitomised that, proudly supporting themselves through their own industry. Each island population was unique and each had developed its own means of trading over centuries, most especially with boats from Napoli, Salerno, Sicily itself, Africa, Greece, the Mediterranean in general and also, Sardegna. The Aeolian island of Salina was the only one that possessed fresh water springs and the land was therefore extremely fertile. In particular for vineyards and the growing of capers. Aurora's father, Agostino Colosi, was a colossus of a man, though much greater in strength and density than sheer height. He was not, as some thought, also with a dense mind. He had single-handedly brought about a change toward modern industry, bringing to light the delectable *Malavasia* wine and more intense *Cucunci* capers. Agostino, with his growing vineyards and ingenious mind, had no time for nonsense. This included the idea of any man who might be stupid enough to go back on their word.

Contracts were useless, they could be broken and were generally necessitated by the *pezzenovanti* of that great city to the north. Though upon meeting Carlo, with his modest boat, affable personality and consistent reliability, the two developed a common respect and kinship. Agostino had sensed in the young man an astuteness that surpassed his meagre front as a fisherman. Carlo also traded in the red coral only available in Sardegna and the finest pearls.

One day, in their usual monthly trading, Carlo had crafted beautiful wares from the coral and presented it as a gift to Agostino. A gesture in appreciation of their continued trade and business. Signore Colosi was taken aback by this familial etiquette, such a gesture was indeed a wise one from such a young man.

His hard character softened, Agostino would not accept a refusal of his offer for Carlo to join him to visit the family home. He was indeed obligated to join the Colosi family for lunch that day. It was late August, 1914 and though this was the main most time for harvesting their grapes, Aurora was also summoned to the house early that day. A young woman, but nonetheless old in her parents eyes, she was now considered illegible for marriage. Thus was her continued presence in her family house since childhood. Her meeting with the young Carlo was positively electric and the lady of the house, Signora Colosi, was not the only one to notice this.

Brought back to the present, Aurora had felt as though she'd recovered with enough energy to walk once more. There was a sudden rustling of bushes and pebbles close by and then a heavy and familiar panted breathing.

Catoi had only just enough energy for thought, spurred on physically by the enthusiasm of what he may be able to achieve. It was time for these arrogant peasants to pay their price for insolence. And it was fine that it came in the form of having Aurora alone with those pretty hips, lips and silky legs. Catoi was astonished to find Aurora sitting under the shade of an olive tree. As he slowly made his way down a small rocky escarpment made into stairs from constant human use, Aurora looked up clearly terrified and frozen. Catoi felt both enraptured to protect her as he would a prize but similarly and disgustingly, ready to perform any manner of acts with her. He felt a surge of enthusiasm and excitement at the realisation that he most likely would receive what he'd set out to acquire.

Aurora could see that Catoi's eyes betrayed one thing only. She hadn't the strength to resist so rather, she equally set out on a plan of her own, to distract the landlord pig.

As Catoi clumsily tried to sit and lay day down on top of Aurora, he fumbled to reach her skirt and as he did he found himself surprisingly arrested by her disarming nature. Indeed, her lightest touch might even contain evil within a demon….what a delectable creature. She insisted she was dirty and said she needed to go home to wash first. While Catoi had stopped and pondered this for a moment, he felt a searing and excruciating pain in his head. Coming to, he realised he'd been given a hard blow to the head, of all people by Aurora's husband Carlo.

Both of them were standing above him looking

down. Catoi, incredulous as to how the hell Carlo had suddenly appeared here, hissed and stumbled for the revolver he had concealed in an inside pocket. It was an old *Bodeo* model from last century but he knew it worked just fine. Before he could load a bullet by the simple thumb click of the loader, it was kicked out of his hand. As the gun was sent hurtling through the air, it landed in a tumble and went off, ricocheting off the rocks that surrounded them, all three of them having reacted by ducking for cover. Carlo knew this wouldn't be the last time such a transgression might be made by their *illustrious* landlord.

So in a short time of a few seconds he'd decided this was Catoi's last day and last minute. Aurora though not murderous, seemed to have read her husband's mind. Possessing a strength Carlo had never seen in her and without words, they picked him up, screaming by his arms and legs. Carlo had positioned himself at the man's legs, lest his wife be given a kick where they would bear children. They knew the rocks would ensure him dead and then setting down into the sea, it might be weeks when he was discovered if at all. They also knew that many people had fallen accidentally into the sea this way and perished. The pig's death would be no different.

While the couple swung him from side to side to gain momentum, Catoi struggled and scratched like a cat. But it was too late. They'd gained an unbreakable synchronous momentum and he knew what they both had decided for certain, that he wouldn't be allowed to live. That these were his last moments. He thought he could see his mother calling from beyond the precipice and despite his incredible efforts at holding onto Aurora and slashing her wrist in the process, he found himself being hurtled outward and suddenly falling, feeling terrible pain for but a split second before everything he knew came to a black stop. The tragic spiral of the Lucchesu legacy had been brought to an unplanned end, through one decisive and fateful blow.

Carlo and Aurora were breathing as if they'd run a marathon, scratches on her arms where Catoi had tried to summon his strength to free himself.

Carlo looked around and suddenly noticed the glint of metal where the old gun lay and decided it best be taken and concealed forever. While Aurora calmly waited appearing frozen at what had just happened, Carlo carefully negotiated a few rocks down toward the precipice of a cliff that overhung the Mediterranean. It's all seeing eye seemed personified with a constant, emerald like glint that reflected continuously, even on sunny winter days. Carlo thought again of the *Nuraghi* people. How many deaths and what secrets did that same Mediterranean sea hold unto itself of those ancient times?

Now Carlo and Aurora would be included in that repertoire of acts committed with nature as their witness. Today's crime was a necessary act. Carlo knew that had he allowed Catoi to live, then things would have certainly worsened toward more tragic results. One where he or his wife might be lying at the base of those craggy rocks instead of Mr. Lucchesu. Regardless, Carlo still couldn't expunge himself from the terrible remorse he now felt concerning even this human life. He felt sick, promising himself that he would avoid murder and indeed violence for the remainder of his life, at all costs. Within himself he prayed to Mother Mary, whom he adored, that she please forgive him and allow him and his wife safe passage to their new life in Abruzzo. That he was indeed sorry for what he and his wife had just done but that it had been a just act of protection and that he and only he, should assume all responsibility for ridding the world of Catoi Lucchesu.

Though these had been committed firstly in self-defence and ultimately pre-empting Catoi's vicious and cruel nature, Carlo felt that he must atone for this life lost for the rest of his own lifetime. That Mary would oversee his self-admonished punishment as he had so asked of her and God.

Carlo pulled the revolver out from under a large boulder, where it had been partially hidden. Holding it in his open hand he looked down sombrely, the gravity of the events that had occurred these last minutes had impacted upon him like a tidal wave and he began to feel a cold sweat and a great nausea begin to take control of his senses. For the sake of his wife, Carlo knew he must not yield to panic or indeed uncontrolled emotion. Thus began an osmosis within the psyche of Carlo Luciano, where tenderness still existed but, where he now buried it deeper into his soul, allowing a clinical objectivity to take its place at the surface of his person. As he looked toward the sea, he kept the gun barrel faced backward and toward the ground. Once again he heard a characteristic whining of the wind that almost sung out of tune. It began as unnaturally abrupt as it had stopped, like a man that had run a marathon to bring him a message, halting rapidly. He was not afraid. As he clenched his eyes shut, he felt he sensed the ghosts of the *Nuraghi* guide him for what must be done; that all, was most certainly not lost.

Stronger and more resolute, Carlo opened his eyes and realised the nausea had dissipated and his heart had stopped racing. Returning to his wife, he laid the revolver gently within the cart under some peaches that hadn't been sold. Tomorrow he would take a quick trip to the sea over an abyssal trench and deposit the weapon into the depths of the Mediterranean.

Aurora, driven by adrenalin, seemed to be completely devoid of pain and discomfort. Her husband, in returning from the rocks just metres ahead of where they now stood, had another look transfixed on his face and person in a way that she had never seen. She had heard the phenomenal wind, a little strange in its strength during the warmer months, it was as unplaced as her husband now seemed, having calmly brought the weapon back and laid it alongside their belongings and produce. Whatever her Sicilian father's misgivings had been about Carlo the Sardinian, he would be proud of the man that now protected her. That no man nor law bar God, would hold debt within him or oppression over him. Carlo walked silently close to her as Aurora, glassy eyed looked up at him in a bazaar admiration.

Another specific facet of love that she had never until this moment, felt nor even imagined of him. Beginning to hold each other's fingers gently until the strength became moderate and then a passionate embrace, caressing each other's backs. Strangely and seemingly out of context, they felt a surge of erotic passion begin to grow and their embrace ensured Aurora's knowledge of that.

Like nothing had happened of the previous hours, the loving couple travelled back to their house and farmland, with Aurora sitting comfortably and cross legged in the cart, while Carlo pushed it slowly, trying to ease the cart over the rocky bumps in the path, minding his knowledge of her sure biological discomfort. Perhaps it was shock that had arrested Aurora's cycle. In any case, a profound change had taken place inside her. Indeed if one life was taken, so too did the way of things see to it that this would be balanced by life, somewhere, somehow. She couldn't possibly be fertile now, yet she sensed it. Aurora clutched the cross her father had given to her as a little girl and wondered if this was another of God's wondrous designs, to help us help ourselves.

While the cart gently bumped over rocks in the coastal path, the couple looked at each other in silence with what were almost exchanged smiles, both privy to each other's thoughts and relieved to be rid of Catoi forever. Perhaps it was the certain knowledge of their having to depart this place definitively which began to incite their love making that through their lustful gazes had already begun.

There was a natural spring at the back of their house, which slowly meandered down to the sea. Carlo lifted Aurora off their cart easily and she placed both hands on his face as she slid slowly toward the ground, deliberately pressing herself against him on the way toward reaching the earth. They paused for a few moments and without words but intense eyes, he led her to the spring.

Slowly and beginning with her shoulders, Carlo undressed his wife and eventually himself. He then gently set about washing her scratched hands and dusty feet. When he arrived at her waist she quivered, at which he began kissing her stomach and hips until he found the warmest part of her. Lifting her leg to allow him further, she pulled his head closer to her and gasped, closing her eyes toward the sun kissed sky.

Standing slowly, Carlo again began kissing her lips as Aurora felt his hardness while bathing him in her gentle cleansing with the crisp, clear spring water. He became much harder and at that, he picked up Aurora once again with ease and care, bringing her into their *casetta* farm house.

Carlo laid his wife down so gently on their bed that she felt as if the gods from the clouds had eased her back on to earth for pleasure. As Carlo slowly turned Aurora, he kissed her back and arms until he finally entered her, feeling an intense heat and wetness surround his member. Aurora turned until she could see Carlo and they stopped for the briefest of moments returning suddenly to their passionate kissing which became harder, until Aurora finally began to weep with bliss and happiness.

That night saw the couple embrace love in a way they never had, where tears had their place and an erotic voraciousness took over with breathless authority, the likes of which neither had ever known.

The seeming change in Carlo's character earlier that day was not lost on either him or Aurora that they felt might one day be delivered to their children, most especially a boy who would become a man.

From the small island of Salina near Sicily and for generations, a legend had been told and also revered by Aurora's father. It was said that a man spawned from the throngs of passion by the relief of an averted disaster, would inherit extraordinary character. One conceived by the balance of an unbreakable strength and love. An individual of purpose where no time was wasted, no words spoken without purpose and everything would be studied for the accumulative arsenal of resources toward the building of an empire. His dedication to his family via any expense, including himself would become legend.

When Aurora awoke, she found herself with a feeling of great assurance together with her satisfaction now turned tranquil. Then, in a way only a woman could know, she realised something had seeded within her during the intimacy with her husband. She felt vibrant in a way she'd never known and realised that she was with a masculine child inside her.

Aurora turned slowly, smiling at Carlo sound asleep and began to tenderly caress his face. She knew immediately what name to give their boy. A name that her father had wished before he passed away. There was a Latin derivative of the Germanic name *Hlodwig* whose namesake was 'fame in battle'. Her father had explained that a man is always at battle in life, mostly to provide for his family in every sense both accurately and wealthily. Thus such a man was no stranger to becoming a great warrior in life. This name was *Aloysius* in the old Golden Latin and in Italian became, *Aloisio*.

Aurora was comforted and reminisced upon the legend that her father had presented to her. She reflected upon the day's happenings with an extreme sense that they had changed the way of things. Fabric, space and time had been flexed with a new destiny. It would begin with her knowledge that the boy to become a man created by her love with Carlo, would be named Aloisio Luciano.

Carlo and Aurora Luciano

In Gratitude

Thank you for purchasing the Advanced reader preview to 'Bianco'. I hope you enjoyed reading it as much as I enjoyed writing it. The full and complete novel is available for Pre-Sale order immediately and discounted until the official launch in May 2018. Bulk orders will attract a further discount.

For reviews, testimonials and more, please keep up with the latest posts at Fb:

Gianni A V Di Camillo.